29 8

1-00

MUSCOVY

by the same author

poetry
MANDEVILLE
DRAGONS
BLIZZARD

fiction
SINGING A MAN TO DEATH

Muscovy

MATTHEW FRANCIS

faber and faber

First published in 2013
by Faber and Faber Ltd
Bloomsbury House
74–77 Great Russell Street
London WC1B 3DA

Typeset by Faber and Faber Ltd
Printed in England by TJ International Ltd, Padstow, Cornwall

A CIP record for this book is available from the British Library

ISBN 978–0–571–29735–1

2 4 6 8 10 9 7 5 3 1

Acknowledgements

Acknowledgement is due to the following in which some of these poems first appeared: *Contourlines, Literary Imagination, The London Magazine, New Welsh Review, PN Review, Poetry International, Poetry Review, Poetry Wales, Where Rockets Burn Through, Whereabouts* (CD). 'Enigma Variations' was originally sent in instalments to the Poetryetc mailing list, and the untitled poem that ends the book was also sent to Poetryetc.

I have drawn on the following sources for some of the poems: Francis Godwin, *The Man in the Moon*; Robert Boyle, *The Aerial Noctiluca*; Edmund Jones, *A Relation of Apparitions of Spirits in the County of Monmouth and the Principality of Wales*; The Powys Digital History Project (http://history.powys.org.uk); Guy Miège, *A Relation of Three Embassies from His Sacred Majesty Charles II to the Great Duke of Muscovy, the King of Sweden, and the King of Denmark*; David Bellos, *Georges Perec: A Life in Words*; *The Pillow Book of Sei Shonagon*, translated by Ivan Morris. 'Macros' is based on three photographs taken with my digital camera, 'Foggy Beach' on a photograph by David Hurn, 'Nocturnes' on three paintings by William Degouve de Nuncques.

I should like to thank members of the Aberystwyth University Poetry Workshop for help and advice, and the Department of English and Creative Writing, Aberystwyth University, for a semester of research leave which enabled me to finish the collection.

Contents

MUSCOVY

The Man in the Moon

I THE GOOSE ENGINE

. . . my only companions a flock of wild geese
that disputed the grass near my hut,
eyeing me when I approached.
They would not be shooed,

but when provoked shrugged into the air,
then folded themselves back down,
the whim of flight passed.

They saw me as one of them,
a flapping biped.

～

The moon rested on the mountain, rock on rock –
you might step from one to the other.
My geese snored, oval cushions
in the goose-white light.

With much time for thought, I brooded on
that icy *noctiluca*:
might one live in it?

Had geese reason? What haven
did they fly off to?

～

Studying their burbling language and coughed cries,
I found no sense there. They would not heed
human words, having no more
than walnuts of brain.

White moved them, and flapping. They would come
to a sheet at my window
for their dole of corn,

fly errands, a full basket
strapped to their strong feet.

~

I rigged the sheet in front, like a spinnaker
(but it was not the wind it would catch)
and hooked my birds to the struts
in a rigid V.

This shape had such urgency for them
they began striving at once.
The frame bucked, lifted,

so I could scarce hold it down
for the leap of it.

2 FLYINGS

The lamb, all legs and nerves, was irked by the ground,
kicked it away. Each time it kicked back
with a jolt that arched his spine,
made him kick again.

[4]

I tied him to the frame. The geese flapped.
The rag-doll face showed nothing.
A bleat blew away,

and for the space of two fields
he treadled the air.

~

Myself weighing no more than a dozen lambs,
Sancta Maria, twenty-five geese
(all I have) might, at a stretch
ora pro nobis.

The grass raced between my hanging feet,
tilted, and fell. I saw waves
swing past my elbow,

my shadow kicking at them,
in hora mortis.

~

A salad of trees, a peppering of beach,
the great blue flecked with goose-dropping foam,
but most of the world is air
no man can live in.

I tugged at the line to yank the sail
and steer my birds to a rock;
small as a limpet,

it fell behind as the geese
strained for the mountain.

~

[5]

Wingbeat by wingbeat we clambered up the sky.
Rock swayed before my eyes. I could read
each crack and blotch of its face,
till we swung over

and my feet dangled on the summit.
We flopped on that cold doorstep
in a field of clouds,

the birds muttering, feathers
still trying to fly.

3 LUNAR PASSAGE

Earth carried on in the gaps between the clouds,
blue and green, fabulous with distance.
How had I lived there? How long
would I be falling?

The lines tensed. The geese rose above me
like a surge of white weather.
It was their season

to vanish into the sky,
and I went with them.

～

Then we were elsewhere. I felt the earth give up.
We moved too fast for breath, but the lines
had gone slack now, the wings stopped.
We were still flying

[6]

in a windless brightness that faded
the stars to milk and water.
Motes sparkled round us:

swarms of cuckoos and swallows
on their lunar flight.

~

Looking back I saw the globe where I was born,
smudged with forests, doodled with coastlines.
That flashing sheet of metal
was the Atlantic.

That pear with a bite out of one side,
must be Africa sliding
east as the world turned,

that oval – America,
just as the maps show.

~

We sailed that lukewarm afternoon that had forgotten
how to get dark, beyond rain or snow,
while the world's engine turned it
twelve times behind us,

and ahead the moon became a place:
the dark patches were country,
furred with trees and grass,

the gold light came from the sun
striking the oceans.

[7]

There was world here also, a hill where we came down,
a thicket of leaves for us to chew,
tasting of green and perfume,
a view of more hills.

The moon's grip being gentle, one leaps
as readily as a lamb,
springing at a thought

to the height of an earth oak,
landing goose-softly.

~

Trees grew tall as a steeple in that lightness,
and the inhabitants of the place
looked down at me when they came
from heads like rooks' nests.

Each carried two fans of curled feathers
with which to flurry the air
and so leap further.

They bowed low and addressed me,
but knew no Latin.

~

How I was taken before their king and queen,
learned the notes of their singing language,
tasted moon food, smoked the sweet blue
of moon tobacco;

[8]

of three gems: a topaz whose yellow
could light up a church, a jet
whose black scorched the hand

and one of no known colour –
all this you shall read,

~

but after the long night with the cloudy earth
shining its almost-daylight on us,
the rising sun was too close
for me to bear it,

so my birds were shepherded away
and myself led off to rest
in a dark quarter.

I woke from my fortnight's sleep,
the full moon waiting . . .

Noctiluca

Robert Boyle experiments with phosphorus, 1680

He swishes a stoppered flask in his fingers,
   the spoonful of wet ash in the base
      the grey of distilled London.
         The rest is only
           tepid air

till the daylight's battened out of the chamber.
   Then the flask's neck crawls with whitish fumes
      that tremble and shine like flame
         and glowing droplets
           bead the glass.

Rubbed on the fingers, this self-shining substance
   gloves them with light, a Hand of Glory
      to make the ladies shiver.
         Urinous vapours
           swarm from it.

He touches it to his tongue. The burning taste's
   not acid or alkaline but some
      empyreumatical oil;
         his mouth throbs with its
           stink and gleam.

Is this what meteors burn with? Or those soft
   after-dark flashes without thunder?
      The spooklights of bog country?
         Rotten fish, glow-worms
           are less bright.

You could float this watery light on the sea,
   to summon the chill spirits of fish,
      or steep a clock face in it
        to shadow the hours
          of darkness.

When the servants have carried out the candles,
   the flask's a lantern at his bedside.
      He cosies it in the sheets
        basks in his phantom
          plasma cave.

It's made of us. Hours of furnace and bellows
   have brewed this lucent dribble and steam
      from 'somewhat of the body':
        what's in us that shines,
          our hot gold.

Corpse Candle

The house was black when I came back from the inn
   down the clogged path, my lantern swinging.
     The door and windows were barred.
       But in the outhouse
in a thicket of cobwebs and rustpocked hoes
   a servant was stretched out on some sacks.

He was shut in his own dark, digging for breath.
   When I shook him he went still deeper,
     where it was harder to find,
       then struck a blockage.
When he resumed the sound was slimier
   and a gloss of wet rimmed one nostril.

What came out was a soft flame, nostril-shaped –
   fat at one end, tapered the other –
     that almost shrank back inside
       then ran down his lip,
and unhooked itself, slipping into the air
   and lapping as at some sustenance.

It meant he would die soon. I had never seen
   the light that throws the shadow of death.
     You may meet it some midnight
       on its way to church,
perhaps in a procession of dark figures,
   fluttering before a waxy face.

No ghostly mourners here, just the animus
   of flame Rhys couldn't keep inside him,

which seemed to nod to him once
and backed through the door.
When I came out it was blinking in the mulch
of black woods at the valley bottom.

I think it waited for me. It did not move
till I'd slithered down the path to it,
for a sign needs to be seen.
I'd heard they were red
but this was merely the tremulous yellow
of an amputated candle flame.

It stopped again at the footbridge, fidgeting
where the loose plank crossed the tarry stream
as if afraid to go on.
The church was beyond,
but some flame of insolence rose up in me
and I picked up one end of the bridge.

It couldn't go then. It jiggled back and fore,
almost blue with rage, and I ashamed
to have hurt so small a thing.
I put the bridge back;
at once it cooled and passed me, striking my neck
a light blow, as with a handkerchief.

I lay as one dead while the light went its way,
tracing the path his corpse would follow
to the grave in a few days.
I woke in the mud
of noon with the usual aches but no burned skin.
This happened, though some will deny it.

Walker

The mountain was mostly fields, rather greener
   than the scraps of field in the village.
      Tilted as if for display,
   they had a jaunty, Sunday-best look.

And the sheep carried on, canted to one side,
   trotting on their adjustable legs
      till my upright seemed askew.
   Only the mountain could set me straight.

The path comforted me with its trodden white.
   It was in no hurry, nosing through
      a wood of shrivelled oak trees.
   The mountain was an ache in my thighs;

nothing to see now but the unreadable
   path in front of my face, a scribble
      of dark wet running down it.
   The view that brought me here was behind.

I turned to see the houses grey as ideas,
   their stone bulk vaporous with distance,
      and, beyond, another slope
   I might have stood on and seen myself.

Strange how soggy the going was. My feet pressed
   a black oil from the spongy surface.
      The hollows bristled with reeds.
   One might drown there, high above the earth.

The mountain was nine parts weather, one part rock.
   Wind blew round corners, shivers of rain
      scurried in at me sideways,
   cloud formed a chilly coat around me.

I was an inkwash of myself, wet on wet,
   among the limp vertebrae of ferns
      and the fuzz of bilberry.
   One stroke would smear me into a blur.

There were syllables in the wind now, Wow up,
   half woman's voice and half hunting horn,
      and I seemed to see someone
   cleaving the bushes ahead of me.

I guessed who she was, though she never turned back,
   by her old-fashioned four-cornered hat
      her dress the colour of ash,
   the apron flung over her shoulder,

the can of milk she carried in her right hand.
   I almost trod on her heel. When I gasped
      she moved off. I could scarce see
   the flap of her through the stinging drops.

She was a crinkle in the outline of rock,
   a shrug of the rain. I would lose her
      at every jink of the path.
   She seemed to wait without slowing down,

her form as watchful as a coat on a hook.
   Seeing her was sure proof I was lost:
      it was she that made me so,
   as she had been all these rainswept years.

I sang a little to myself, as you do
   when the weather is full in your face,
     felt in my belt for my knife,
   knowing she hated the sight of steel,

and flicker by flicker she faded away
   till there was only dusk, and below
     one petal of cottage light.
   She is known on the mountain: beware.

Familiar Spirit

A knock at the door, one-knuckled, no louder
   than a fall of ash from the chimney,
     scarcely more than a loose thought
       tapping inside your skull,
     except that it is outside,

and now it's a social knock, two syllables,
   hallo, *shw mae*, a neighbour's upbeat,
     downbeat, doorstepping rhythms
       that just want to take
     a couple of your moments,

and why are you sitting in the reddening
   gaze of the fire when the door wants you
     over and over, tripled,
       quadrupled, Harri,
     a fusillade of wanting,

till you can't help but get up, shaking your head
   as if all your thoughts had got loose now,
     cross to the source of noise, put
       your hand to the latch,
     Harri, and open the door

to the greying wind of an autumn evening
   that doesn't mind if it does come in,
     sure it's not disturbing you,
       no more than the blank
     rectangle of the doorway,

for there was no one there, Harri, no one much,
   but whoever there was is in now,
      and you hear a creaking sigh
         as of one settling
         into a chair by the fire

across the semicircle of glow from yours
   to listen to the comings and goings
      of twig and dry leaf that sound
         more urgent at night
         as if in the room with us,

and when you climb the ladder to go to bed
   in the smoky space under the thatch,
      don't drop your tallow candle,
         if a hoarse voice says
         goodnight, Harri *bach*, sleep well,

for there is plenty of room for both of us
   in the cottage with its pressed earth floor,
      its rafters where crooked tools
         hang next to the hams,
         both maturing together,

and even if you lie all night, eyes open,
   inside your cocoon of candlelight,
      there's such a thing as morning,
         when light is all round,
         and voices come with bodies

that you can ask back to watch with you tonight
   and make their nervous jokes round the hearth,
      while I lounge in the oven,

[18]

loving warmth myself,
and when I speak, Harri *bach*,

with an oveny echo like a dropped pan,
see how they jump back as if the fire
had spat a hot coal at them,
when all I said was
Won't you introduce your friends,

then dozed off in my genial confinement,
for I have a cat's liking for sleep,
waking, catlike, at odd times,
to walk in the dark
and overturn a few chairs,

perhaps, brushing up against your old fiddle,
to play a strathspey or scrap of hymn
for the squeaky joy of it
like a door singing
to itself in the small hours,

for what's the use of a cottageful of night
if no one sounds out its resonance
apart from snoring in it,
which you do, Harri,
although you claim you can't sleep,

because one can become used to anything,
even a what-shall-I-call-myself
that snuffles around the floor
or throws something soft
with a whump against the wall,

and when your big toe stuck out of the blankets,
   too sugar-mouse-pink to seem like yours,
      so that I had to pinch it,
         what made you gasp was
         the smallness of the assault,

but then I can grab you anywhere I like,
   even that squeeze of lane by the church
      where I bumped into you one
         frost-breathing evening
         to whisper a neighbour's news,

Harri, they're coming to get me with a gun,
   and next thing I knew they were treading
      their mud into your earth floor,
         overcoats crammed in,
         the man with the gun wrenching

the long barrel free and trying to aim it
   not to kill anyone visible,
      and myself egging him on
         from all sides at once
         with a shower of pebbles

that flew through the gaps in the air to bruise him
   leaving his friends untouched, though it's true
      I left dents in the cupboards
         and the cottage strewn
         with drifts of makeshift shingle,

but all was calm afterwards when that woman
   with the graveside manner sat you down
      at the table, held your hands,

and with her eyes closed
raised her voice to the cobwebs,

asking me who I was and how I came here
to this clutch of whitewashed stone houses
the far side of the mountains,
had I ploughed here once
or fished in your sunken sea,

had I no family to remember me,
no grave to put chrysanthemums on,
queasy personal questions
that made me shudder
all the way through the table

to think of that sugar-mouse flesh I had once
and its hangers-on of arms and legs,
hair, toenails, parents, siblings,
its love for others
pink and straggly as itself,

which took all the shine off this candlelit house
with its smell of dust, woodsmoke and damp
where I'd frolicked all winter,
bullish as the wind
that I heard charging outside

on its way to batter some other village
and its poor householders, that I hear
now as I unhook myself
from hearth, walls, eaves, door,
saying thanks, Harri, goodbye.

Cwm Elan

Sheep stare from bone masks, totter away
on stiletto legs, bearing the weight
of their dirty curls. Cold for July,
just the all-year yellow of the grass
for sunlight, a desert gone to seed.
I round the hill's shoulder. Down below
a curve of Rhine appears,

half-hidden by forest and shining
a continental blue at the sky –
the illusion held there by a dam
that stops one lake swallowing the next
and overseen by a prim folly
of turret, like a Hornby castle.
These are the reservoirs

where they keep the nineteenth century
in a thin medium of water:
a church and its weed-bearded parson,
a dim shop where sweets crust in the jars,
and the wheel that turned it all, sawing
timber from the slopes, grinding the corn.
Men talked by the warm kiln.

The barenecked poet launched a toy boat
on the mountain streams, a cat on board
with a face the same shape as his own.
He brought his new bride to the old house
with two hundred acres and a ghost
to live among rocks where the waters
were shallow, the air deep.

Then came the dam-builders, a village
of men and what comes with them. They posed,
deloused, disinfected, sleeves rolled up,
with their stonecrushers and windjammers.
Beer to be drunk in moderation.
A school for their children, the dancing
Elan Valley Snowflakes.

Gone under, dissolved, overwritten.
When they took down the village, they forgot
the plank store where they'd bought steel buckets,
blankets and doormats. As the lake rose
it bobbed to the surface, wallowing
among treetops. They hauled it ashore,
baptised it a chapel.

Now there's a bench instead, where I sit
watching the discontented mirror
break and reset itself. It's nothing
and holds the gaze the way nothing does,
one lake on the brink of another,
lapping at the sill, waterfalling
in a fizzle of white.

That couple were haunted by water.
Harriet drowned in the Serpentine,
Shelley's body was dredged from the sea
and heaped among beach wrack to be burned.
But here one summer the level fell
and the stones of the old house reared up,
dripping, into the dry.

Muscovy

I FROM LONDON TO ARCHANGEL

There are leagues of waves to cross first. We set forth
in July, when the days will hold all we need:
ships, men, ropes, swear-words, stinks, the sun above all,

beds, chairs, two trumpets, twelve footmen, a chaplain,
six pages, a chirurgeon, one more fellow

who can dip a pen, write our way in and out.

~

What's green to us now? We rest our eyes on fields
made of the same blue as the sky, soft going
for those who have become part of the weather.

This day a plump cavorting around the ship
as if on purpose for our entertainment.

Too smooth for the sea to hold, the fish squirt out.

~

Where we went rose and we climbed up it. We fell
from the sea's brink and crashed into our old selves
maundering where we had left them. We were still

falling, climbing the seething deck as we lay
where the horizontal was lost in darkness.

O let us stay where we are so we can drown.

~

[24]

A grey cloud on the sea that does not move. Watch
and it will harden. All we have lost is there,
green and grain, smoke and warmth, crevice and footing,

but the wind wills otherwise. Sixty leagues south,
and the bowsprit broken, we pass Newcastle.

Crocked in port, we sulk. The days sail on their way.

~

Then the wind turns. The ship crawls from sea to sea.
This one is white at heart, glazed over with blue.
Each headland nods to the next, crouched beneath firs.

A spring of fresh water, sweet as liquorice.
Filled three tuns therewith, ours being corrupted.

Cut down a cross on the beach to make a fire.

~

This is where we must start from, a place with wings,
where the churches have the heads and beaks of birds.
Roofs ride at anchor, bits of sail drift over

and the archangel city rests from its flight
where the Duina disembogues into the sea.

We have been here three weeks. Where did you get to?

The firs grow thick as grass. Wolves and bears live here.
In the sweltry glades the flies hum like your thoughts.
Light sets them in amber. Shadows net your feet.

Clinker-built towns, boardwalks raised off mud and dust,
founder in the first whitening of winter.

Time to steam by the stoves, wear furs from the wood.

~

They eat deer, boar, hares that turn white in the snow,
ducks, geese, such small birds as scarce make a mouthful:
fieldfares, thrushes, larks. The woods are full of bees,

whose honey, beaten in warm water, makes mead.
Mulberries, rasps. The land's too cold for walnuts.

A salt black jam, the eggs of a Czar of fish.

~

In this close hut they bake you till your hair hurts.
You thought you knew how to sweat, but not enough.
The splashed stove hisses and white vapours choke you,

till beyond naked you glisten on the bench,
a residue for lake water to dissolve.

At last you rise from the grit, and drip. Drink this.

~

A bear would have more grace than these men who dance
as if they no longer know where the ground is,
hopping from foot to foot, drunk on strong water.

Four men braced on a wooden platform, swinging
high as a windmill. Two women seesawing

one each end of a plank, in a flap of skirts.

                    ∼

A straight blade, curved at the end, fixed to each sole:
shod thus they slice their way on the frozen lake
in polite haste, bending the knee right, then left.

So they race forward, wind scathing their faces
and the water's carapace fending them off,

the air fraught with a noise like war, scrape and sing.

                    ∼

They find God in the dark, in the ache of legs
as they stand hip to hip and mutter, in the priest's
great dome of a voice. They cross themselves, bobbing

before a brown face, hooded and haloed, sunk
in an oaken twilight, whose candlelit eyes

look down, to one side: love does not meet the gaze.

3 FROM ARCHANGEL TO MOSCOW

There are versts to cross. We set forth while the snow
is still heaped in the clouds, and the river flows.
No fire on board: you must cosset the person

in marten, sable, fox or beaver, and sleep
shivering on sheepskin in the furry dark.

The men heave and the wet rope lifts. We move off.

~

We walk in the late sun. Our barge walks with us,
hauled against the stream. A wolf on the far bank
dissolves in shade when we arrive with our dogs.

A skiff brings a village priest bearing presents:
a hen with its eggs, autumn-red gooseberries.

We moor by the stars, our men's fires in the woods.

~

A skin of ice shushed by the hull, the first snow
grits in the air, tasted when you have to breathe.
Then flocks of it pressing round us. No comfort

in reindeer drawers and coats of hide worn bearlike,
fur outside. We crouch below decks, listening

to the scratch of ice, the slow smash of our way.

~

The sledge is a boat of bark, lined with coarse felt.
First you must lap yourself in furs, stop each chink,
for the air is your enemy. You stretch out,

cuddling a flask of *aqua vitae* for warmth.
The carter, behind his horses, quickens them.

The world is rolled up tight, glides on with no sound.

~

The cold finds you in your sleep. You flee from it
the way one does in dreams, not touching the ground,
across a flatness that is always the same:

firs flicker against the snow, nights against days,
as you hurtle lengthways through your drowsiness.

There are no ruts, no rocks. You dream your way there.

~

It was a clear night when we passed through the gates
to the squawk of the Czar's trumpets. Rags of light
littered His Lordship's sledge dressed with white bearskin.

His Lady followed him in a glass-doored sleigh,
and footmen, chirurgeon, pages, in their furs

sat stiff in the gleam, slid in state through the streets.

4 THE EMBASSY

The King's gifts are sent on by sledge: chests of cloth
for a land of fur, two gold watches, three clocks,
two pairs of pistols, a hundred pigs of lead.

My Lord's in costly black for his audience,
turning a diamond-banded hat in his hand.

In the Great Hall as they rise, the shrill of silk.

~

The Czar gives his hand to be kissed. One by one,
My Lord first, we climb the throne's steps. A boyar
holds up the hand under the weight of kisses.

Ruler of the Great, Little and White Russias,
Emperor of Astrakhan, Lord of the North,

his brown eyes soft in the sharp light of his jewels.

~

Nine hours of feast. At last they brought in small trees
of a dark candy, each branch gilt at the tip.
It seemed we had not escaped from the forest.

My Lord and His Czarskoy Majesty drank toasts
till a scarlet syrup puddled the table –

blood from the Czar's nose. My Lord thanked him and left.

~

It thaws in the streets. The crowds press to the church,
palm leaves held high, as if the coming of spring
transplants the land. The Czar kisses a gold cross.

There are more kisses at Easter. The people
make gifts of hen's eggs, curiously painted

red, blue, green, with rings and stars. They boil them first.

~

We roost in our house. The words fly back and forth:
trade rights, the ancient love that links our two lands,
precedent – our words squeaked out with a limp quill

in curling Latin by the man His Lordship
appointed to write them, one Mr Marvell.

He wrote us so far. Now he must write our way out,

~

for we can make no sense of this place. We miss
the swards of hedged park with their deer, the oblong
manor house, the rain's smart clip on the gravel.

In London the King listens in his chamber
to the manifold ticking of the Royal clocks

and waits for news. But there are leagues to cross first.

Macros

SAND

There used to be a game,
those chunky polygons
impinging, exploding
on the black screen of space.

But it's air that keeps these
niblets of asteroid
weightlessly jockeying,
and sound can reach us here –

the sh of the smash as
tumbling objects collide,
crystalline vertices
snapped off with just the sigh

bare feet press from a beach.
Saltgrains, glassmotes, coalseeds
roughhousing together
to make what we call soft.

HOTTENTOT FIG

It's not what you think, this
sunhead nestling among
unCornish foliage,
a gold disc, a smile badge,

parched mat on a hut floor,
sand-dune blow-in, displaced
Atlantic African.
Look in its face, eye, heart

at what you thought was veldt.
Greenish feelers, writhing
Mandelbrot curlicues,
sprout from a bed of goo.

If a plant can have such
juices, tissues, organs,
animal volutions,
there's no dry in the world.

ANT

I had not seen it there,
stooping to photograph
shinlevel undergrowth.
Feet hooked on a pink sail

of vetch, it waves a prong,
clambering upward, one
scimitar mandible
soiled with a speck of sludge,

and rides the pitch and yaw
of canvassy petal –
magnified thicknesses
with a scurf of white hairs,

while from deep in the small,
unsuspected, this hot
astronomical sphere
glares out at me, an eye.

Sea at Low Tide

It has frittered itself away in rockpools,
turned itself into a mist,
a sandshine,

and lost its voice. Whatever it had to say
it swallows. There is only
the hushed gulp,

while a bird flies round with a looping whistle
like someone trying to find
its wavelength.

Poem in Sea

Saturday

scrambled

sunrise

slate

she

shingle

shells

spray

soufflé

step

sea's

stores

storms

swallows

swamps

sandbars

early

egg

extends

expanses

explores

entangled

earache

ebullient

each

encro

elemental

energy

electrifies

explorers

empires

engulfed

a

apricot

across

above

among

algae

air

as

awkward

aching

amorphousness

and

atmosphere

aviators

archipelagos

Atlantis

spans

Spitzbergen

Sumatra

silver

Severn

sustains

sharks

s

stl

salmon

sinks

sounds

spotlight's

she

sleep

s

s

Easter

Eddystone

effloresces

emerald

Euphrates

eels

er

ess

es

egg

evening

expand

eye

emb

e

e

e

and

and

amethyst

arrogates

Amazon

abalone

a

andca

a

apparition

already

a

arcs

arks

a

a

a

[37]

Foggy Beach

Once the sun's gloss had been
taken away, only
porridgey anklechill
and the lean folds of waves

on miles of ridged and wormed
hardcore remained. Hauling
lopsided bucketfuls,
we kept on with the work

this flat land asked of us,
never even doubting
barefooted drudgery
was what we had come for,

while those who'd sought a tan
reclined among beachtrash
absorbing fleshily
the soft white of the day.

Enigma Variations

a)

†t the sign of the †pple
he sold p†rrots fished from the rivers
th†t flow out of P†r†dise:
his windf†lls.

b)

%etween %um and %osom,
%um and %alls,
%alls and %osom:
well-%alanced %odies.

c)

Read lightly over these words.
Under their ‡urling roots
lies William ‡axton.
‡lose the book after you.

d)

The printer's $evil
hurling his spear at the wrong key
cleaves S from hea$ to tail –
$olorous stroke!

e)

Op©n th© ©nv©lop©
and light ©xplod©s
©v©rywh©r©.
©!

f)

Deciphering the }locks overhead
as they }
o}}
out o} it.

g)

Been sittin' here all evenin',
watchin' the 'nats, spittin'
'obs of phle'm and writin'
silent letters to my 'irl.

h)

Don't drop your £s, £enrietta.
We don't want to £ave
some aspiring £arry
gracing his £eirs with t£em.

i)

Don't ask how often
_ got la_d or how many
g_ns _ caught my feet _n.
Assume the hor_zontal.

j)

New Year's Day. The bird
leads him zigzag through the woods.
Door of the old chapel,
a/ar.

k)

The woolball twitches on the rug,
lips snip patterned syllables,
and numbered needles ¬nit
all that I am ¬not.

l)

" "andaff, " "anon,
"and of my fathers,
I know every e" " of you,
he snorted unconvincing"y.

m)

Emperor ...aximus,
acceded AD 1000,
noted for the length of his rule,
...arried?

n)

Beyo|d bears, seals
a|d the trappi|gs of the |orth,
a| i|visibly fi|e li|e
with the su| i|ching rou|d it.

o)

After his Address t^ a Table
the grammar b^^ks were changed
t^ include the v^cative.
^ Cicer^!

p)

It is raining.
All men are mortal.
Therefore acce∴t my ∴ro∴osition
before I catch my death.

q)

How many years chasing its tail?
Why? In which chapter
does the §uesting Beast turn round to face him?
Who eats whom?

r)

He~e the ~ive~
un~ive~s itself,
becomes estua~y
and unp~onounceable.

s)

Cur&ed to go on it& belly
con&piring in whi&per&,
to tangle endle&&ly
plural and po&&e&&ive.

t)

Read ligh¹ly.
Alan ¹uring
res¹s in ¹his box,
¹aken to bi¹s.

u)

Looking for bea<ty, finding yo<
in what is <r, s<b, <n,
next to nothing,
at the back of the q<e<e.

v)

After the ∞olcano,
dice cup, flagon,
oil jar, loaf,
still li∞es.

w)

>hy not our o>n >eatherfronts,
our o>n >ords?
The >inds al>ays blo>
from some>here else.

x)

Loveletters
that don't add up,
a map of where the treasure was,
a love ≠ed out with a single keystroke.

[44]

y)

Unsolved m#steries
number twent#-five,
the #eti. Don't miss number twent#-six,
wh#?

z)

It was free°ing when he arrived
at the sign of the °ebra, heard
from the dark inside
the sound of snoring.

Perec Suite

drEAm

You dodge through the dim tunnels, fleeing the killer locust;
you drop from the empty deck into the shivering reflections;
you smell the crumbled white, woodsplinters, Dettoled floors
of the old formroom; you open the kitchen door to the visitor
who died on you once before, who's returned to get it right.
They've got you for the next eight hours, these flickerings,
while the furred outline in the corner of the bedroom stirs,
her eyes open, seemingly puzzled by her snippet of lucidity.

picturE

A photograph: man with cat. Cat's half-turning away, staring
back at us across a soft spring of body, its Os of curiosity
lacking both colour and blink. It sits on a ramp of cardigan
that tilts as if to hold it up, or as if this listing man is
a Long John just off his ship who thinks his cat's a parrot.
Man's all hair, thick curls on top, patriarchal bush on chin
and a shyly triumphant look as of a magician in mid-flourish
who without knowing how has drawn a cat from a waft of silk.

nIGht

Halfway between one day and the next the town's orange gloom
suffused the room as he woke. He could hear cars on the road
and, much nearer, the belated footsteps of someone left over
from the day before as they trotted to catch up. Even closer

[46]

the wood of the house stretched and the current hummed where
an unthought-of gadget stayed on. Now he was awake the drops
began beyond the glass. They seemed to grow rather than fall.
He got up and looked out at the dark street. What was wrong?

GO

His turn. He fingers a white disc and places it with a click
inside the grid. A cluster is taking shape there, its skirts
beaded with black, but the pattern is unfinished, changeable
like curled steam in the sky. (They're playing in a garden.)
A game takes weeks in Japan, but here they are, half-filling
the summer day with it. A fly lands where lines meet. Leaves
make their dark play against his pieces. When he leans back,
he can't see where it ends, chequered green, dappled armies.

YOU

The one who's looking for something, going from room to room
lifting and leafing, drawing drawers, capsizing shoes, as if
a simple beneath or between might fix it. The one who thinks
that lying on the bed with a naked opposite for an afternoon
may at least reveal what sex they are. The one who frittered
too many bits of self into the word-grinder, gave them away.
Who might have been me and isn't, might be a part of speech,
a twist of the pen. Who was a person once, and went missing.

Things That Make the Heart Beat Faster

After Sei Shōnagon

Her world is wood and silk, the slow weight
   of twelve unlined silk robes hung on her,
      the thick brocade on top, sleeves falling
         in coloured layers: grape, cherry, white;

boards that speak as she moves through the dark
   between one night and the next. She sleeps
      cushioned on wood, adrift in her clothes,

      kneels behind her silk screen listening
to the man who's come to flirt with her.

         ~

Straw mats. A go board. A chest of clothes.
   A fan. A flute. A comb. A cushion.
      Her world is portable. Move one thing
         and everything else changes round it.

There's no glass. Wood slats let the wind through,
   or a crow's retched cry from the garden,
      multiply rain in her head at night.

      Braziers glow in the morning cold.
By noon they're burned out, a frost of ash.

         ~

Things that should be short. Things that have lost
    their power. Winds. Herbs, shrubs. Things that gain
        by being painted. Things that are near
            though distant, distant though near. Insects.

Things that make one feel clean: a clay cup,
    a metal bowl, a rush mat, the light
        that plays on pouring water, the wood

            of a new chest. Unsuitable things.
Birds. Shrines. Clouds. Things that bring back the past.

                            ∼

All night, door to door, the sound of feet
    that stop, shuffle, then move on, as if
        testing the floor for a response, its
            give. A known footstep pauses outside.

She is a room, a door, the stretched skin
    of her mind that a finger taps on.
        She mustn't speak, but she can rustle.

            Listen: his fan chivvying the air,
or is it? All these men, all these rooms.

                            ∼

What's small and makes its home in the dark?
    Threads of leg on her face, the hairline
        sound of a mosquito in the room,
            baby mice wriggling in the corner.

She looks in a cat's ear, sees a gnarled
    grey badland of peak and ridge and chasm.
        Its eyes are gold. The Emperor's cat

                                            [49]

in its ribboned headdress outranks her
and knows it as it twists from her hands.

~

Things that fall from the sky. Rain. Hail. Sleet.
　　Snow that pitches its tent on the ground,
　　　　scuffs the cypress shingles of a roof,
　　　　　　even the houses of the peasants.

No lamps at night: the world is a moon.
　　He swings one leg on the wooden brink
　　　　of the veranda. They talk till dawn.

　　　　The ladies build a mountain, hodding
raw snow in trays. How long will it last?

~

No room in bed for them all: him, her,
　　their words, the tussle of silk. At last
　　　　she wrenches herself free and gets up.
　　　　　　Darkness. An unlined robe. She shivers.

The room cracks its joints. Now it's the size
　　of a palace, the shape of a man's
　　　　breathing. Animals scratch at the walls.

　　　　He has the covers clenched, mollusclike,
in the deep place she can't get back to.

~

Still dark when she hears him snap his fan.
　　He is breathing his way round last night's
　　　　dropped belongings one curse at a time,
　　　　　　doing himself up for the daylight.

[50]

A man should know how to leave, she thinks.
  He ought to be enwrapped in it all,
    their bedding, the last few whispered words,

    till the temple gong shivers outside
and he shrinks to the chill of his clothes.

                    ∼

Sun, night. Melt and freeze. A day of rain.
  The snow mountain grows tired. Its crags wilt.
  The skin is pocked, shrivels. Hollows form,
    paths become waterfalls. Will it last

ten days? More? They kneel in the state rooms
  the ladies weighed down by hair, their teeth
    blackened against the glare of a smile,

    and banter weather. The Empress says,
she says. The bet's laid. The thaw goes on.

                    ∼

She loves duck eggs, wild pinks, the last word,
  shaved ice with syrup, the cry of geese,
    a dawn wind blowing through the shutters,
    the purple trousers of night wardens.

She hates the touch of flies' feet on skin,
  the way workmen gulp their rice, a hair
    stuck to her inkstone, a heron's hunch.

    She has forgotten her scented robe,
puts it on now, still sweet. She loves that.

                    ∼

For him night's not done. He walks door by door
   through the dimness. He has to send her
      a twist of poem, a pinned flower.
         A woman's waking behind her screens

in her silk nest. He stands at the edge,
   smiles. She is warm from last night, waiting
      in her corner for her own poem.

      Her orange robe, his purple trousers,
hot coals in the ash light of the room.

                    ⁓

She brings cakes for the man in the hut:
   this heap of grey ice is my mountain –
      keep the children from climbing on it.
         The gardens emerge from their whiteness,

raked sand, rocks, the wrenched poise of a pine
   hairy with green, but her plan still holds.
      A basket of snow for the Empress,

      with a poem of modest triumph:
I made this out of what does not last.

                    ⁓

To wash one's hair, put on a new dress
   (for no one) makes the heart beat faster.
      To sleep in the fragrance of incense.
         To see sparrows feeding their fledgelings.

Now the last snow's gone, smashed by the men
   sent by the Empress to win her bet,
      to be thinking he won't arrive now

      when the shutters rattle her awake
with a shock of flung grit that's just rain.

Nocturnes

NOCTURNE IN THE ROYAL PARK, BRUSSELS

Left, right, straight on, fawn paths
separate grassbeds. This
modular labyrinth
blues to a fur of woods

a few blocks down that, when
approached, resolves into
identical uprights.
If you are lost, it is

your own muzz you're lost in.
Everything's ordered here,
illuminated by
white blobs hung from the trees,

as if they'd known you'd jump
their palisade, explore
their geometrical
night with its glut of moons.

PEACOCKS

Swags of fir hold night in,
mothball it underneath
hefty material,
make a space where the birds

can scratch in the soft floor,
unsheave their tailfeathers'
radiance, shivering
the starched lace in the gloom

that drains the blues and greens,
leaving these silvery
nightgowned apparitions
like the ghosts that scared you

as a child – not the dead
but ruffled gatherings
of haberdashery
with eyes sewn in the skirts.

THE PINK HOUSE

This is the long night called
the nineteenth century,
cultivated darkness,
the stone lamp of a house.

Its flame shines through the walls,
reddish. Outside, crouching
between rhododendrons,
you watch the blinds light up,

a few stars in the black
foliage, like sugar,
granulate overhead.
Some have spilled on the lawn.

A lodge or a new wing
invents itself, windows
emerging sullenly.
No one will let you in.

The flesh of this house glows
with a familiar
boneshadowed abstractness:
a torch pressed to the palm.

Was

1

The wallpaper was a forest of fishbones.
The dressing-gown was a shroud against the door.
A given moment was marked off by headlamps.

It was still too early for any ghosts.
This area of night was inhabited.
A colourless woman was walking down the street.

The dark was dangling under the lamp-posts.
A settlement of moths was pitching its tents.
There was a consortium of trees, consorting.

The house was next to a dormant canal.
There was an extra blackness where the trees were.
The railway was shuttling lights to London.

2

It was expected that you would gallivant.
It was quite possible to pretend to play.
I was knocking my house down with a tennis ball.

A car was falling apart in a bamboo thicket.
I was picking up pages of book in the grass.
A house was tangled somewhere hereabouts.

The canal was so green you could ride on it.
The water was like Guinness with a green head.
Marsh gas was proddable out of it with a stick.

There was a hedged garden with silver birches.
I was shouted at there by a sudden woman.
It was hard work pretending to be a child.

3

My father was an artist in marzipan.
His egg-shaped head was visible through the crowds.
He was courtly, and called girls Miss in shops.

The war was still within range of anecdotes.
There was a hundred-pound sack of flour, and a rat ...
He was cured of 'Gyppo guts' by eating oranges.

His top speed was twenty-eight miles an hour.
The light in the shed was the colour of new wood.
He was failing to make the evenings into a boat.

He was fearless with puns and boiling sugar.
The table was a Cézanne of candied fruit.
An icing submarine was his masterpiece.

4

Morning was broken by my mother's singing.
There was a pigeon that sang one note five times.
The air was popping with rifle fire from Bisley.

The weather near the school was made of screams.
Outside was a grey area for jostling in.
Playtime was guarded by rhymes and stringy elastic.

Inside was an experiment in formica.
Maths was a jackstraws game of coloured rods.
The queasy smell of plasticine was on me.

The road home was clustered with enemies.
It was impossible to look burly while slinking.
I was practising the vowels that would make me tough.

5

This was when knees were worn in the open air.
The pavement was not your friend, nor was the winter.
When it snowed I was allowed to wear leggings.

Cabbage was cooked everywhere at once.
Curry was pacified in its circle of rice.
Wine was a sweet gold opened at Christmas.

The TV was afloat on a sea of fuzz.
It was switched on early to let it breathe.
The end of it was a diminishing star.

The typewriter was shaken by bouts of Xs.
Interference was more general in those days.
At night the radio was seized by foreigners.

There was a neighbour, high up in the city,
who was swinging on the banister of his office
when the whirlpool of the stairs was his nemesis.

There was a brown dog who ducked out of the leash
once too often, and was lost in a strange town
where there was a shouting man in every garden.

There was my father who lay with his eyes closed
on the floor as if he was looking at something
that was hurtling towards him from the inside.

And there was what passed for me at the time,
who was left behind in the greens by the canal
but was there when I last looked, and still is.

Phonebox Elegy

No one noticed them leaving
as no one had noticed how
every evening
at some almanacked hour

they must have switched on in the twilight
their introverted glow
of dashboard and luminous watch.
Never quite part of the street,

they just seemed to appear
with that Close-Encounters
hovering look
when you'd searched for them long enough.

And you stood in the chilled
belljar of light
and mimed your lifestory
to whoever was waiting outside.

More compact than a church
and less subtle in its demands for money,
it was a heavy-doored
shrine to the invisible,

censed with breath
and the smell of breathed-on plastic,
absorbing our prayers –
'Pick it up. Pick it *up* –'

also forgotten wallets,
chewing gum,
the phone numbers of vice girls
as impossible as archangels,

and the occasional urge to desecrate it
by urine, evisceration
or the cramming in of too many bodies.
We were translated there.

Moth

Call it the night butterfly,
an after-image of the day's blues and reds,
with its sleep-friendly fabric,
its wings squiggled on
in the language of the unconscious,

or call it the candlefly,
scratching at the glass with its whiskers of leg,
fusing with lightbulbs, smashing
its wings to chalkdust,
seeking the flame that makes sense of it.

What Rain Means

I've heard it say sorry over and over
when it hasn't done anything wrong. Sorry.

Other times it's impatient, drumming its fingers,
but won't say what it is it wants you to do,

which you can't do anyway, trapped behind glass
while it paces up and down the street, waiting.

Being shut out suits it. That's when it speaks
with its usual show-off onomatopoeia.

If it tells you it loves you it doesn't mean it.
It says that to everyone, just wants your attention,

would play with you but it has no sense of fun,
has a point to get across, forgets what it is,

but whatever it's saying it says it a lot,
maybe a million times. And that's just tonight.

Streetlamps

Then there was more night
than we knew what to do with,
so we went into the street,
which had been waiting for us
all that time,

or if not for us,
then for anyone to come
and understand its spaces
the way the lamps do in their
cones of gaze.

We walked between them –
veiled sisters leaning over
their patches of ordinary
and making the moths sparkle
with meaning –

till what we said was
strung out in the same rhythm,
sentences left for the lights
to look at, and, in between,
our dark steps.

White ice naps the empty road.
Move on, old nightnurse.